# District Sales Manager: How to Raise the Sights of Each Sales Person on your Team to 6 Million Dollars a Year With a 20% GP

Category:    Business & Economics

Description:   A District Sales Manager, DSM, is the unknown soldier in the industry. Responsibilities are huge and resources are nonexistent. You will see how effective a salesperson can become when you raise the sights of each salesperson on your team to 6 million dollars a year at a 20% GP.

Author and Publisher:     Bob Oros © 2020

Keywords:    District Sales Manager, Foodservice Sales Manager, Bob Oros, Distributor Sales Manager, food-sales, Distributor DSM, distribution sales manager

ISBN:  978-1-300-20998-0

# Table of Contents

## The Unknown Soldier

A DSM is the Unknown Soldier in the industry.
Responsibilities are huge and resources are nonexistent.
This information is geared toward helping you maximize
your efforts and get amazing results from your team.

A successful DSM must have the right combination of
experience and street smarts. You must also have
complete knowledge of not only selling strategies, but how
to train, manage and motivate your sales team.

Implement the strategies in this book and the sales in your
district will skyrocket!  .

## Your DSR's Blueprint for Success

Following is a blueprint for taking a new or underperforming salesperson and giving them step by step training to succeed as a foodservice sales rep.  Teach them these 36 steps and you will be building them into highly profitable salespeople managing a TEN MILLION DOLLAR TERRITORY.

1  Your first day as a DSR

2  The pressure is on to generate sales

3  I may not be cut out for this

4  Multiple call close type of selling

5  Replacing lost customers

6  Continuous prospecting is imperative

7  Start with a marketing plan

8  YOU are the advertisement

9  The number of ad exposures

# 1 Your first day as a DSR

There are many aspects to managing a sales territory. In this section of the book we will address many of them, however, every individual territory is unique and needs to be taken into consideration.

The main mis-conception about how to operate a business is the idea that all you must do is go out and make enough calls and someone will buy. This may have worked at some point in time; however, things are different today.

It's Monday morning. It's your first day on a new territory. You have been assigned a geographic area to work. What do you do?

This is the point where many new salespeople get discouraged. They may have gone through a company training program that teaches them how to enter orders. They may have had extensive product training along with training on warehouse operations, delivery schedules, etc. That will all be valuable information, but what happens when you go out and start cold calling on people who have no interest in buying from you.

As you start walking in the back doors of restaurants, you find that you run out of clever things to say, because you are not getting any response. Your prospect list is getting smaller and smaller because you have been back 3 or 4 times and they still don't show any interest in buying from you.

What should you do?

## 2 The pressure is on to generate sales

You start to run into the same objections over and over again. "I'm happy with the company I am buying from."

"The sales rep is a friend of mine."

"I have no interest in looking at anything new."

"I tried your company before, and it was a bad experience." "Your prices have always been higher than everyone else." You get the point.

You may have been lucky, and the company gave you a few customers to take care of.  They total to a "drop in the bucket" compared to the amount of sales you need to generate a decent income.

The pressure is on.  You need business NOW.  You are now three months in from the day you started. You have been running around your market like a chicken with their head cut off.

WHY ISN'T ANYONE INTERESTED IN BUYING FROM ME?

You begin to wonder if you are cut out for being a sales rep for a distributor. If you are a seasoned salesperson, what did you do at this point in your career?

## 3 I may not be cut out for this

The doubts are starting to add up. You begin to get discouraged.

You begin to think about how great it would be to have a place to go every morning. You think about other types of sales jobs you could be working at.

For example, I could sell cars. That way the customers would come to me and all I would have to do is close the deal.

Maybe I could sell real estate. That way I wouldn't have to call on companies who are being called on by salespeople all the time.

Maybe I could get a job in retail. That way I show up at the store every morning and wait on customers who have already decided that they need to buy what I am selling.

Getting in the car and driving around all day calling on people who won't even throw me a bone is getting old.

Your sales are pitiful and when you look at the successful salespeople in your company you wonder how they do it. It seems like they all had a lucky break. They have a better territory with more customers.  They are located closer to the warehouse that gives them advantage.  They have been around a while and started selling at a time when it was easier.

For you veteran salespeople who are listening we need your help. What did you do to overcome this doubt?

# 4 Multiple call close type of selling

I am going to break it down and give you a step-by-step plan for becoming a top sales professional. Following there will be many lessons that you must learn and implement.

You are in a unique type of selling. Most of the generic type of sales training is focused on the single call close type of business.

That is where you sit down with a prospect, go through the entire process from beginning to end, close the sale, get paid, and never see them again.

In our business, it is just the opposite. It may take several calls just to get the prospect to agree to listen.

What can you do to break through this wall of resistance?

How can you build a relationship with a potential customer if they won't even give you one minute of their time?

If you have had these thoughts, and the thoughts from the previous lessons, you are not alone.

If you are a veteran salesperson and have joined the ranks of those who make a very good living selling food and supplies to foodservice operations, my hat is off to you. You are one of the elite.  You are one of the few who have the tenacity to stay with it, even if you had many days when you asked yourself what you  were doing in this business.

# 5 Replacing lost customers

Many times accounts are lost because of reasons you have no control over. Here's the top 10 reason you lose accounts.

1. They go out of business.

2. The new chef/cook uses a favorite supplier.

3. Their credit becomes shaky.

4. Your company drops a product line.

5. The purchasing office moves to another city.

6. The purchasing manager is transferred.

7. They decide to purchase all products from a bid.

8. An order gets messed up and you can't recover.

9. New owners take over the restaurant.

10. The owner changes purchasing responsibility.

These 10 reasons point out the importance of keeping your funnel full of prospects. When one goes away for one of the above reasons, you should have several you have been working on to find a replacement. Prospecting calls should be an important part of your process.

As we go forward, you will be given a precise plan on how to organize your time and market area for continual growth.

# 6 Continuous prospecting is imperative

Do I really need to prospect for new accounts?

The answer is YES.  If you plan to increase your commissions, to make selling your career, or to be promoted, you must prospect for new customers.  Even when sales are good, you need to be aware that the situation can change quickly.  You must replace the accounts that you lose.

The foodservice industry has the highest customer turnover rate of all businesses.

Turnover means you may not be able to recapture the business. Prospecting will shape your success or failure as a sales rep. To evaluate potential customers effectively, you must keep updated information on prospects.

You must start with a base.  You have been given a geographical area to work. It may be a section of a city, or it may be in the country where you must drive several hours a week to visit the entire area.

Well before you make that first Monday cold call we discussed; you must do a lot of homework.

# 7  Start with a marketing plan

The very first step, before you start trying to knock on doors and sell food and supplies, is to establish a market.

This is where most salespeople fall flat. They start with no concrete goal.  They start without a sound marketing plan. You might be thinking - "But my job is to SELL, not to do marketing."

Marketing is a huge part of managing your territory. What if your company had a $50,000 monthly marketing budget and you were promoted to the VP of Marketing for the company.  What would you do?  What would your plan be? Would you dump it into social media?  Would you take out TV ads?  Would you do radio commercials and put ads in the local newspaper?

That wouldn't make any sense, would it? Restaurant operators are not going to call you up and tell you to stop by and pick up an order because they heard your radio ad on the way to work.

What about direct mail? You could send letters to all the prospects in the market. Would that work? No.  It has been tried by sales managers who didn't understand our business and failed big time. Thousands of letters were sent out without ONE response.  Not ONE!

So what is the answer? How do you put together an effective marketing plan for your marketing area?

# 8 YOU are the advertisement

It takes many exposures to get an advertising message across and it results in a sale. It takes even more exposers to have someone become a regular customer.

Your thinking has been conditioned in the same way. You have been "sold" the ideas and self concepts you have. You have never been given a specific guide to the sales AND marketing process required to become highly successful in the concept of business to business sales. Also called B2B sales.

If commercial marketing alone could generate sales, a salesperson would not be necessary. Even if all the orders were entered by the customer, not the salesperson, there is still a need for the type of "marketing" we are talking about.

You have to launch an important marketing campaign to your customers! You must use a positive marketing campaign that will replace their old belief with new positive ideas and concepts. You must tell them over and over again what you expect of them. You must dwell on a successful outcome, not on their reasons why they won't buy from you!

In the next lesson I am going to give you the power. Knowing and applying this power will enable you to finally understand the concept we are talking about regarding marketing.

## 9 The number of ad exposures

Why do you see the same TV advertisements over and over again? Here's what happens each time you are exposed to an advertisement. This is from the American Marketing Association.

1 You look at an ad and don't even see it.

2 You see it again and still don't notice it.

3 You are aware that it is there.

4 You have a feeling you have seen it before.

5 You read the ad.

6 You resent seeing it again.

7 You start to get a little irritated with it.

8 You start to wonder if you're missing out on something.

9 You begin to think you should take a closer look.

10 You ask your friends and associates about it.

11 You wonder how they are paying for all these ads.

12 You start to think that it must be a good product.

13 You start to feel the product has value.

14 You remember wanting a product like this.

15 You start to want it.

16 You accept the fact that you may buy it.

17 You make a note to buy the product.

18 You wonder if you can afford it.

19 You make a mental decision to buy it.

20 You buy what the ad is offering.

21 You become a steady customer.

## 10 The number of personal exposures

Let's look at what happens each time a customer is exposed to YOU. 1 They look at you and don't even see you.

2 They see you again and still don't notice you.

3 The customer becomes aware that you exist.

4 They have a feeling they have seen you before.

5 You catch them at a weak moment, and they talk with you.

6 They see you again and feel resentment.

7 They start to get a little irritated with you.

8 They wonder if they're missing out on something.

9 They begin to think they should take a closer look.

10 They ask their friends and associates about you.

11 They wonder how you are paying for all these visits.

12 They start to think that you must be a good person.

13 They start to feel that you may have some value.

14 They remember wanting to deal with your company.

15 They start to become friendly and want to do business.

16 They accept the fact that they may give you a try.

17 They agree to fill out a credit app.

18 They wonder if your prices will be higher.

19 They make a mental note to give you a trial order.

20 They go ahead and place a small order.

21 They continue to order and become a steady customer.

## 11 Why don't people buy

Trying to complete a sale within the first few exposures is a shortsighted and undisciplined approach to doing business.

Here's why:

2% of Sales are Made on First Contact

3% of Sales are Made on Second Contact

5% of Sales are Made on Third Contact

10% of Sales are Made on Fourth Contact

80% of Sales are Made on Fifth to Twenty-first call

If there's one thing that too many salespeople are bad at, it's consistent exposure. It's the same old story—you don't want to be annoying, so you play it safe. But you need to develop a follow-up strategy that will get you more clients and help you open new accounts.

Why don't people buy?

There are many reasons why people who could benefit from your product, service or expertise do not buy. At least not without further marketing, including:

1.      Inertia.

2.      Lack of time.

3.      Too many other things on their mind.

4.      Concern about cost.

5.      Cash flow.

6.      Budget constraints.

7.      More pressing matters.

8.      Your failure to do enough "marketing" to establish your name in your market so they'll buy without question.

## 12 Number of customers

Now it's time to determine how many customers you need, and what their potential is, to reach your sales objective. If you didn't understand the information we discussed so far, I would suggest you go back and review it.  Better yet, let's review it now.

1 You think selling food is going to be easy.

2 You think all you have to do is knock on doors.

3 You have old beliefs that don't work in distributor sales.

4 You think marketing is someone else's job.

5 You don't realize that YOU are the marketing department.

6 You never realized how many exposures it takes to sell.

7 You didn't realize 80% of sales are made after 21 contacts.

8 You were taught that after 3 calls you should give up.

9 You never realized how ruthless the competition is.

10 You never knew there were so many reason for not buying.

11 You never realized how important relationships were.

12 You didn't realize this was a higher level of selling.

Now that we have a much clearer concept of what our job as a foodservice sales professional is, let's go back to that first Monday morning on the job and take a more realistic look at what we have to do. Let's move on to carefully selecting a customer/prospect base.

## 13 Selecting a customer/prospect base

Before we come up with an exact number of customers, let's work backwards. Let's start with the end in mind. Using this formula, we can determine your precise future income.

If we could look inside the workings of your mind, we would discover it is a goal seeking device. It works like a goal seeking missile, or like a GPS. Give it a crystal-clear target and it will automatically direct your actions towards achieving that target. Notice I said it must be crystal clear. It cannot be vague, just as the destination you put in a GPS must be exact.

You might be thinking you already have a clear goal. "I want to achieve a 10% increase over last years sales."

When you give that number to your mind, what happens. Your mind starts asking for more information. Where is that increase going to come from. Should I open new accounts? Should I look for bigger accounts to call on? Should I focus on selling more categories? It becomes too confusing. Besides, last years numbers were not all that impressive, so a 10% increase is going to end up being mediocre. How does that relate to your commission? Who knows!

To get a good answer to the question of how many customers you need you have to go back to marketing.

The old style of distributor sales is fast becoming obsolete. Your responsibility is expanding.  You must think like a company owner. You must have the ability to present your sales and marketing plan to your sales manager as a company president would present their business plan to the bank in order to get a loan.

Would your current plan persuade the bank to give you a loan to keep the company going, or would they say, sorry.

## 14 The step-by-step process

Let's break this down into a step-by-step process. We will start with an overview and then go over each step in more detail.

Step 1: You must be calling on enough customers and prospects whose total purchases are ten million dollars.

Step 2: To accomplish this you must start going through any current customers and prospects and determine what their total annual purchases are.

Step 3: You must list these customers and prospects on a spread sheet along with their total purchases.

Step 4: You must keep going until the total purchases in the customers and prospects total $10,000,000.

Step 5: You must determine if the list of customers and prospects are a good fit for your company.

There are more things to consider, but for now let's go a little deeper into these five steps.

## 15  Getting enough exposure

Step 1: You must be calling on enough customers and prospects whose total purchases are ten million dollars.

Why is this important?  If you have 10 customers and doing hit or miss prospecting, you will fail.  You will spend too much time redefining your territory, running in all directions at the same time and become confused.

You will not see the big picture. Every week you will go out and restart your 21-exposure program. You will be too tempted to give up and settle for a few scraps of business here and there. You will be developing shallow relationships that never have a chance to grow.

The spreadsheet of your sales that your company provides is only a small part of the picture.  Yet, that is all you have to go on. The company spreadsheet showing your sales for last week does not represent what you are doing.  This is a problem that only you can fix.

Remember we talked about the importance of marketing? This is where your true skills as a salesperson will be revealed.

If you are exposing yourself with consistent "marketing" to ten million dollars worth of purchases, what do you think will happen?

If you apply the 21-exposure advertising and marketing law to customers and prospects on a consistent basis, what do you think will happen?

When you are doing your marketing and prospecting calls, you are building towards the future. How much information can you get into a 2 or 3 minute, carefully crafted, commercial. When you are in this phase of the process with a customer, you can't expect them to stop what they are doing and give you an order on the first or second call.

## 16  Total annual purchases

Step 2: To accomplish this you must start going through any current customers and prospects and determine what their total annual purchases are.

This is easier than you think.      Once you start looking at any type of foodservice operation through the eyes of a food professional, whether you sell this type of customer or not, you will be able to estimate with surprising accuracy. Here is a few examples, just to get you thinking:

You visit a nursing home with 100 beds and a daily meal allowance of $3.00. This gives us a daily cost of $300. Times 365 days their total purchases are $109,000.

A prison you visit has 150 inmates and a staff of 30 for a total of 180 meals a day. The daily allowance that is spent outside is $1.60 per day.  That is a total of $288 per day, or $105,120.

A family restaurant is serving 1500 meals per week with an average check size of $8.50, giving us weekly sales of $12,750 or $637,000 per year. With an estimated food cost of 35% the total purchases are $223,125.

A retail deli with weekly sales of $3,815 will have a "product cost" of 60% and will be purchasing $119,028 per year.

A sandwich shop selling 150 sandwiches per day with an average check size of $4.90, will be buying $80,482.

A hospital with 100 beds and a 70% occupancy rate and 30 staff meals per day will purchase $116,800.

## 17 Total annual purchases

Step 3: You must list these customers and prospects on a spread sheet along with their total purchases. As you are building your list and making the first investigation call you should estimate the total sales and total purchases.

The average check size is relatively easy to determine by looking at the menu. Pick out two or three of a restaurants' high- volume items for breakfast, lunch and dinner, add the cost of a beverage and throw in a pro-rated amount for dessert and you will have produced a number that will be surprisingly close.

The second number is the estimated meals per week. Although the owner may be reluctant to reveal this figure, the chef, kitchen manager or buyer may not. Simply ask them how many meals they serve in a week. If this doesn't work, count the number of tables and chairs and estimate how many times they turn each day. A casual conversation with a waitress can be very informative about the number of turns in a time of day.

Once this estimate is in hand, the math is straightforward. For example, an operation that does 1,000 meals per week and has an average check size of $6.50 will do $6,500 in weekly sales and

$338,000 in annual sales; if they do 3,000 meals per week with an

$8.00 check average, they're doing $1,248,000 annually; and so on. This step seems basic, but it goes a long way in showing what opportunities, or lack thereof, a prospective account has.

Next, estimate the food cost at somewhere between 25% and 35%, depending on the restaurant type, multiply it times the sales and you have their purchases.

Keep doing this until you end up with a total of ten million dollars.

# 18 The heart of your business

Step 4: You must keep going until the total purchases in the customers and prospects total $10,000,000.

How many accounts is this going to take to total ten million? It depends on your market area; however, it will be somewhere close to 50. That is a manageable number and it will be about average.

This list is the heart of your business. If you end up with 50 customers and prospects, the average annual purchases will be about $200,000 per year per customer. If you are already a seasoned sales rep and you are calling on 70 or 80 customers, you are not doing your job the way it was meant to be done. It's not your fault. It's just that the concept we are talking about has never been presented to you.

If your average comes in much lower than that, a red flag should go up. You are either calling on all small accounts, or you are underestimating the potential of your accounts. If your average is around that number, you are calling on some good accounts with a lot of potential.

If your customers can barley meet minimum order, they may not be the type of customer you want to invest all your time and effort in. There is a natural tendency to think small when it comes to restaurant purchases.

Consider this; a family with 4 or 5 children with purchase double your minimum order every two weeks. With that in mind, how much more does even a small diner purchase?

Why is this the heart of your business?  Because it shows you the POTENTIAL of your market. I am not suggesting that you can get all this business, but you are at least thinking about the opportunities rather than the limitations.

# 19 Are they a good fit

Step 5: You must determine if the list of customers and prospects are a good fit for your company.

As you are screening and selecting your customer/prospect base, you must make sure they are a good fit for your company. You can't be all things to all people. You must identify your strengths and admit your weaknesses.

The industry is divided into many different segments. You must match your inventory with the type of customers you can service.

For example, are you strong with country clubs, family diners, sandwich shops, and Italian restaurants? Are you weak in healthcare, Mexican restaurants, and Chinese restaurants? Knowing this will help you make sure you are not setting yourself up for failure.

In the next section of the course we will explore the various segments, but for now, look over your list of prospects and make sure you can take care of them with a certain level of confidence.

For a veteran salesperson this is common knowledge learned through trial and error. With a new salesperson this can be a challenge. Without any previous foodservice selling experience, you may believe that you can sell anyone.

There are certain product categories that are used by nearly all foodservice customers. For example cleaning supplies and paper products. However, you don't want to limit yourself by being a fill-in supplier or a secondary supplier, you want to keep your eye on the prize. To become the main supplier in your 50 customers.

If you are calling on a ten-million-dollar market and you have 35% of the total business, what will your sales be?

## 20 Three-million five-hundred-thousand

let's do some math.

With a $10,000,000 market you KNOW there is plenty of business on the table. You are no longer scrambling around looking for prospects. You can put that number in big letters above you desk.

Right below it you can put your goal - the percent of business you want to capture. Depending on how long you have been selling, it could be 10% or one million, it could be 30% or three million.

You have done all the homework. You can now focus on putting each one of the customers through your funnel going from prospect, to credit app, to first order, to increasing specific line items, to becoming their main supplier.

But here is the key. You must apply the marketing program we discussed. You must consistently and persistently call on these accounts. You must gain their trust. You must be sincerely interested in their business. You must bring them samples. You must bring them ideas.

In other words, you must act like, and become a
CONSULTANT.

Now your mind has a clear goal, like we discussed.  Like
entering your destination into your GPS, you are giving
your mind a clear path to getting there.

Now you can even give your mind an affirmation, or
mission statement, to work on:

"I am going to call on my TEN-MILLION-DOLLAR-MARKET
AND I WILL SELL THEM THREE-MILLION-FIVE-
HUNDRED-THOUSAND THIS YEAR!"

## 21 Take it to the bank

Let's give our plan the bank test. If you were the president of the company and you had 10 salespeople, what would your presentation look like? Here it is:

We are building our sales team from 10 to 20 highly professional, highly motivated, salespeople.

Each salesperson has or will have a market of TEN-MILLION-DOLLARS annual potential.

That gives us a total market of TWO HUNDRED MILLION DOLLARS.

Some of our salespeople are new and are selling between 10% and 15% of their TEN-MILLION-DOLLAR MARKET.

Some are in the middle and are selling between 20% and 30% of their TEN-MILLION-DOLLAR MARKET.

Some are on the top of their game and selling between 30% and 50% of their TEN-MILLION-DOLLAR MARKET.

As a company we currently have 10 salespeople and are selling 50% of our ONE HUNDRED MILLION DOLLAR MARKET.

Our goal is 20 salespeople each calling on $10,000,000 in potential business with the goal of capturing 50% of that market.

50% of 200 MILLION DOLLARS IS 100 MILLION PROJECTED SALES.

If you were the bank, would you invest in this business?

Put this sign above your desk: TEN-MILLION-DOLLAR MARKET My goal is THIRTY-FIVE-PERCENT

## 22 Making the calls

Out of 2,347 salespeople during a one-year period, 1,482 of them failed before the year ended.  That equals a 63% failure rate.

The reasons for this high rate of failure?

97% Lack of industry

37% Discouragement

12% Don't follow instructions

8% Product knowledge

4% Dishonesty

2% Poor health.

Think about it! 97% of the people who failed simply didn't do the work! And the work is making calls.

Show me a person of average ability who diligently gets out of the door early every morning, works the sales and marketing plan we discussed, contacts 10 to 12 customers or potential customers every day and I will show you a person who is destined to succeed.

There are plenty of people who know how to put in a good day's work. You are most likely one of them. I know several salespeople who are in the five to ten million dollar a year arena. Ask any of them how they can sell so much, and they will tell you the same thing. They work their tail off! They are hungry and ambitious.

The point is each marketing area is unique. Each territory has different circumstances and different types of customers. Each territory has a different competitive situation.

If you want to start selling more it may be time to look at that number of accounts you are calling on.

It may be time to consider implementing the sales and marketing strategy we discussed in the previous lessons.

Remember - 97% of sales people fail because they don't make enough calls.  Implement the 50-account 10-million-dollar market plan and you will succeed with scientific certainty.

## 23 Desirable selling qualities

Let's look at a few more numbers. A research firm sent questionnaires to 300 purchasing managers in various lines of business.

The questionnaire made the request that each person should set down the two or three qualifications he or she believed more essential than any others for a good salesperson to possess. The following list shows the qualifications needed by salespeople in order of their importance.

26% Product knowledge

16% Hard work

17% Sincerity

13% Honesty

07% Personality

07% Tact

04% Presentation ability

03% Ambition

03% Education

This is helpful information for you as a salesperson. It helps put together a priority list for what to improve on. The first one is the most revealing, 26% product knowledge, proving that you can't "wing it" with a chef or restaurant owner – you must know what you are talking about.

You also must be sincere, meaning that follow up and doing what you say will make a big difference on their decision to buy from you. This is something that cannot be avoided even if you think it is not necessary.

And hard work (making prospecting calls and follow up calls) is what it takes to get and keep the business.

As you build your territory, the first selling job is to sell yourself on the 50-account 10-million-dollar-market. If you know your products, are sincere in what you say, and make the calls, you will succeed.

## 24 Whatever-it-takes service

Here are 2 quotes from the president of a distribution company given during an interview as the reason they shut down and went out of business.

1. "Willing to do what-ever-it-takes to serve the customer doesn't have value anymore."

2 "Doing business based on relationships is just not as highly valued as it used to be."

I have some serious concerns about what he said!

As bad as I hate to see anyone close, I think these reasons are thin.

Let's take a closer look and see what we can discover. Let's look at this from the customer's point of view.

1. Service: "What-ever-it-takes to serve the customer doesn't have the value it used to have!"

Immediate, enthusiastic and energetic response to a customer request is more valued today than it has ever been. The problem is salespeople have become so dependent on technology that the secret of good customer service has disappeared! Passion for service is more appreciated than it has ever been, because it is so rare!

The best salesperson is always the one who responds with massive action in the face of a problem - that is "what-ever-it-takes" service.

It is not only impressive, but it leaves a trail of trust behind. Not the best talker wins, it's the one who gets the job done. The best approach to building customer service is to deserve confidence.

The next lesson we will discuss the value of relationships..

## 25 Highly valued relationships

2. Relationship: "Doing business based on relationships is just not as highly valued as it used to be."

If you think relationships are not highly valued, try doing business without one. Just the opposite is true!

If I am your customer, I am not going to pay a higher price because of our relationship, but you will get to keep my business if we have a good relationship and you don't take advantage of it. When your company has a special price on something and you don't offer it to me because you know I will buy it anyway, is that a relationship or are you just using me to pad your gross profit?

If a competitor comes in and offers me a lower price on something that you have been overcharging me on, is that taking a relationship seriously? It seems to me that a relationship is a two-way street. I give you my business and you take care of me.

I have every competitor in the market calling on me begging for my business? Do you think I am going to turn them away while you are calling me on the phone for your order and they are bringing me samples, specials and ideas?

From a customer's point of view the relationship must be stronger than ever before. It has to be sincere. It must be beneficial for both the salesperson and the customer.

Here's the bottom line.    You have to do things the hard way - you have to go back to SELLING! You have to get back to making face to face contacts with your 50 customers and prospects (that's called service), bring your customers VALUE and some good reasons to TRUST you so you can build a good relationship.

## 26  Setting your sales goal

Just imagine the strong relationships you will build if you keep calling on your base. Where do you want to be 1, 2 or 5 years from now?

Keep in mind that you are building a career, not just keeping a job.  You can earn a lot of money and get a huge amount of satisfaction by working the 50-account 10-million-dollar market plan.

Once again, the important thing to remember is that in every carefully selected 50 foodservice operations there will be more than ten million dollars per year in purchases. If you are just starting out, the first objective would be to sell them 10% of their purchases. The second objective 20%. The third objective 30%. The fourth objective 40% and - fifth objective 50%. Fifty percent of 10 million dollars is FIVE MILLION IN SALES!  What would your commission be?

50 Accounts = $10,000,000

1st level 10%          1,000,000

2nd level 20%          2,000,000

3rd level 30%          3,000,000

4th level 40%          4,000,000

5th level 50%          5,000,000

The trust that is necessary between buyer and seller is not something that can be built in 3 or 4 high pressure sales calls. It sometimes takes years.  If you call on an account four times per month, the first year you have seen that person 48 times.  By the end of the second year you will have seen them 96 times, the third year 144 times and by the end of the 5th year you will have seen them 240 times. It is impossible to implement this kind of persistence and not become an outstanding success.

## 27  Building an activity sales plan

How to make use of the "Law of Averages" by making a sufficient number of sales presentations.  Here's how you do it...

Select a product category each week, make a "signature presentation" and present it to all 50 of your accounts.  This gives you a reason to stop in and see your customers.
This is the "marketing" part of your job.

One presentation per week - Delivered to 50 accounts = 2,500 exposures in 50 weeks

If you took the time to develop one new sales presentation per week and deliver it to 50 accounts, it would be a grand total of 2,500 per year. This is using the law of averages to your benefit.  By making each call more productive and focused, the results will be much better.

Remember, 26% of your customer's decision to buy from you is based on product knowledge.

The secret of becoming a product expert is to focus your selling efforts on a single product category for an entire week. By taking the category of hams and presenting your line of hams to all your accounts during the week, you will learn more about ham than you ever thought possible.

If you repeated this program every week you would not only become an expert in each product, your customers would see you as a resource.

## 28  Create a routine

The next 9 lessons are specific things you can do to better manage your territory.

Create a routine. No matter what you are working on, create a routine. Block times for specific activities and stick with the plan. Turn your calendar into a bunch of blocks and put activities into those blocks. Whatever is not planned, you don't do. Customers appreciate and count on salespeople who are consistent with their schedule.

Stop Multitasking. You may think you're being more productive, but studies have shown multitasking slows you down. Your brain can't do two things at once. When you think you're multitasking, your brain is darting from one task to another in rapid succession. As a result, you lose 40% productivity because the brain is constantly shifting gears and trying to focus. Not only does multitasking kill your efficiency and performance, it's harmful. Prioritize your sales activities and focus on one thing at a time.

The 2-Minute Rule - If it takes less than 2 minutes to do, just do it.

We're all subject to something called completion bias, meaning we like the feeling of checking things off a list. So if we make our whole day about lists, it's easy to check off a bunch of easy stuff, feel a sense of accomplishment and then look back on a whole day wasted on busy work. Many small, simple tasks don't deserve the energy to enter them into the system or put them on a list. These tiny tasks get magnified once we start treating them like projects. If something comes up in the day and it just takes a couple of minutes, don't schedule it: just do it.

## 29  Finding prospects

Before you can really evaluate and qualify potential customers, you must locate the foodservice operations in your territory.

ONLINE DIRECTORIES. There are many headings here which list your potential customers.  Check both the yellow and white pages.

NEWSPAPERS. Look for possible prospects in newspapers advertisements, restaurant reviews, or feature stories. Don't overlook weekly food sections.  Newspapers can also give you leads on new buildings being constructed and on renovations. Many run legal notices of new business applications.

LOCAL GOVERNMENT OFFICES. You can get information on construction permit, new businesses, and liquor licenses at local government offices.  In Canada food operators must be licensed and registered. This information should be available.

CITY DIRECTORIES. At many local public libraries, or at the Chamber of Commerce, you can obtain city directories of foodservice establishments.  In the directories, you will have to look under a  variety of headings (restaurants name, hospital, etc.) to gather information.

MEMBERSHIP DIRECTORIES. Directories from various trade associations such as the local Restaurant Association, the Hotel / Motel Association, the Chefs Association, and the Dietitians Association can provide you a wealth of prospective customers.

TERRITORY SURVEILLANCE. Research and contact will not do it all. You need to keep your eyes open continually as you move through your territory. It is much easier to use freeways than to drive the back roads. The easiest route, however, may not always be the most profitable.

## 30 A territory map

Begin by making a list of every foodservice operation in your territory and by recording all information that you can obtain about each operation. You can keep the information in an Excel spread sheet, on file cards, in a notebook, or a software program.

The important thing is to develop a system of recording and updating prospect information which you can use in your prospecting efforts. This information will give you a good idea of just what kind of prospects you have.

Keep in mind you are looking for the top 50 customers in your market. You may have to do a lot of searching to find them.

A territory map - either electronic or on the wall.

Set up a map where you can insert pins showing the locations of current customers. Use a different color pin to mark the locations of prospects. A territory map has several advantages.

First, it shows you where your largest concentration of prospecting time should be spent.

Second, it helps you locate areas where a new customer might help you balance out your territory geographically.

Third, the map gives you an idea of the route you are currently taking, and it may show you ways to rearrange your territory and make better use of your time.

## 31  Delivery

With today's high cost of running a delivery truck, efficiency in routing is extremely important.  There can only be one "first stop" on a truck. Yet on any given day, there can be no fewer than 10 requests to be the first drop on certain routes.  If you have put an in-town delivery on the tail end of an out of town truck you can rest assured that you have just ruined the efficiency of that route for the day.

When gathering intelligence, always ask about delivery requirements. It's better to under promise and then exceed expectations than it is to have a situation where your beeper goes off and you discover there's an upset customer calling to find out where your truck is.  A delivery set-up that will permit your company to meet its goal to be the low- cost supplier and help you avoid headaches is ideal.

There are a lot of trade-offs that come into play here, so keep an open mind on delivery requirements.  A "C" customer whose order would help fill out a half-loaded truck that has to make other drops nearby anyway might be of great value to your company.

Make a note of any special invoice requirements. Some customers require that certain items such as non-foods, meats or dairy be broken out and invoiced separately.

You'll want to get a feel for how your prospective customer handles the receiving process. Does this operator carefully check in each order when it arrives and settle any differences at that time? Or does the customer look like the type that scribbles their signature on the invoice without even looking at the shipment, only to call you back three days later, claiming there was a stick of cheese missing and expecting you to give them credit.

## 32  Customer files

G-2 refers to the gathering of military intelligence.

This process can work equally well in helping you, a foodservice salesperson, develop your territory.

Gathering intelligence on your customers as well as keeping notes and a copy of their menu is important information to keep in their file.

For example, what type of buyer are they?

There are basically two types of customers: those who buy on price and those who buy on value. As soon as you walk into the kitchen, you can tell which of the two you are dealing with.

Price buyers. If the place seems messy, disorganized and even potentially unsanitary, you are looking at a price buyer. When you go into the office,  you'll probably see a stack of bid sheets showing weekly quotes from every distributor in the market.

Value buyers. On the other end of the spectrum we have the value buyer. In this instance, the kitchen will be organized and clean, the office will be neat and orderly, and the operator will usually have an open mind toward new ideas.

Every time you learn something new about a customer, or when you read something that will be of interest to them, put it in their file.

Before making your next call, make it a habit of reviewing the file the evening before you make the call.

## 33 Calendar

Using a sales calendar properly can make the difference in whether a you meet your sales goals.  Here are 5 tips that help organize your time.

1.      Keep your calendar with you at all times. This can be an electronic calendar such as one on a smart phone or a hard copy such as an organizer. You never know when you might get a call that requires a scheduled meeting.

2.      Schedule it now. If you know you need a meeting, get it on the calendar as soon as you can. The longer you put it off, the more likely you are going to have scheduling issues or conflicts.

3.      Put customers first. If you're asked to do something by a customer, put it on the calendar so you don't forget. Always schedule a follow-up meeting after each presentation.

4.      Schedule time in your calendar for email. This is perhaps THE most important calendar management tip. You can easily spend hours on email if you allow it.

Dedicate a specific time of the day to email. Unless it is an emergency, don't let email (or social media) interrupt your productive selling time.

5.      When is your productive peak?  We all have an optimum time of day when we're the most productive. For some, it's the first thing in the morning.  For others, they get their second wind right after lunch. Do you know when yours is?  Pay attention to your productivity peaks and schedule customer meetings during those times. Schedule that time  on your calendar for making cold calls or visit prospects.

## 34  The Golden Hour

The last hour of the day can be your most productive time for planning.

In B2B sales, the last hour of the day gives you a chance to look back at all the hard work you put into the day, and plan for the next day.

On your calendar block out the last hour of the day from any other meetings. During this hour, take the time to step back and do the following:

1.      Review The Day – First, look back at all the meetings you had that day. Think about what was accomplished, what you owe your prospects and customers as far as information, and what next steps you will take to move the business forward. This is a key time to evaluate what went right, what went wrong, and what you can do to move toward  achieving your goals.

2.      Review The Next Day – After reviewing what happened today, look forward to the next day to see what is coming up. Prepare for your meetings taking place that

day by doing research on new prospects, preparing information and pricing for calls.

3.      Update CRM and files – One of the most crucial things that gets missed in sales is keeping consistent notes and next steps updated in your CRM. This will help you remember each conversation you had with a prospect for future calls and later follow-up.      Also, file any information you collected during the day and put it in the customer's files for future discussion.

4.      Update your list of things to do - It may be beneficial to have two lists.  One that you need to get done tomorrow, and the other for you longer, ongoing projects.

## 35 Managing your projects

Did you ever hear of the single idea where a consultant was paid $25,000?

The president of a large steel company had granted an interview to a consultant named Ivy Lee. Lee was telling the president how he could help him do a better job of managing the company. The president told Ivy Lee that what was needed wasn't more knowing but a lot more doing. He said, "We know what we should be doing. If you can show us a better way of getting it done, I'll listen to you and pay you anything within reason you ask."

Lee said he could give him something in 20 minutes that would increase his efficiency by at least 50 percent. He handed the president a blank sheet of paper and said, "Write down the five most important things you have to do and number them in the order of their importance. Put the paper in your pocket.

The first thing tomorrow morning take it out and look at item number one. Don't look at the others, just number one, and start working on it. Stay with it until it's completed. Then take item number two the same way, then number three, and so on, till you quit for the day."

"Don't worry if you've only finished one or two; the others can wait. If you can't finish them all by this method, you could not have finished them with any other method. And without some system, you would probably take 10 times longer to finish them and might not even have them in the order of their importance. Do this every working day. After you've convinced yourself of the value of this system, have your managers try it. Then send me your check for whatever you think the idea is worth."

In a few weeks, the company president sent Ivy Lee a check for $25,000 with a letter saying the lesson was the most profitable, from a money standpoint, he'd ever learned in his life. This was the plan responsible for turning a little-known steel company into the largest independent steel producer in the world in less than five years. The idea of taking things one at a time in their proper order and staying with one task until it's completed before going on to the next.

Without a doubt, this is the best way to manage your projects.

# 36 Customer complaints

1.      Let them state their case.  Don't interrupt. The
person is geared for talking.  Until he has said his piece, he
is not tuned for listening. If you want your own ideas to be
heard, learn to listen first to the other person.  Ask the other
person to repeat his key points is valuable when the other
person comes to you hot under the collar. Merely letting
him get it off his chest goes a long way to reduce his
feeling of hostility.

2.      Pause before you answer. This will let the other
person know that you consider what he has said of enough
importance to "think about it," or "consider it."  A light pause
is all that is needed.

Pause too long, and you give the impression that you are
trying to evade giving a definite answer. If you must
disagree with a person, the slight pause is important.
Come out with a fast "no," and the other person feels that
you are not interested enough to take time with his
problems.

3.      Don't insist on winning 100 percent. Most of us,
when we get into an argument, attempt to prove that we

are totally and completely right, and the other person is wrong on all points' Skillful persuaders always concede something and find some point of agreement. If the other person has a point in his favor, acknowledge it.  And if you give in on minor and unimportant points, the other person will be much more likely to give in when you come to the big question.

"Yes, I can see you have a good point there, but have you considered this. . . ."

"Yes, I can understand why it might appear that way, but on the other hand..."

## Motivating salespeople

**Most sales teams can be divided into 3 groups**:

**1. Salespeople with less than 3 years in the business.** These folks are overwhelmed by the huge learning curve and difficulty in actually opening new accounts and adding line items to accounts they may have been given. This group is so focused on the day-to-day activities they lose site of the big picture and their inspiration weakens. Many of them don't stick it out.

**2. Salespeople with 3 to 10 years**. These folks have had some success and, as a group, are your highest producers. They are motivated by their own success as well as their increased product knowledge. Their confidence is steadily increasing, and they have sorted out many of the myths about selling, especially as applied to foodservice sales. Even though, as a group, they are producing the largest percentage of your sales, they are still only working at about 60 to 70 percent of their true potential.

**3. Salespeople with over 10 years**. This is where you find your superstars who really see the opportunity, but also this is where you find your "maintainers." These maintainers are the ones who are satisfied achieving the minimum company sales objective and many times shift into a defensive mode. Rather than being challenged by their colleagues who excel, they find excuses to justify their position. Their sales are a valuable part of your overall plan. And every now and then some of them catch the vision and catapult to the status of superstar.

What is the solution, the key that will unlock the potential of your sales team and get them excited about reaching their potential? The answer is to take a new approach to motivating your sales team.

Here is what I mean. Let's say you have 50 salespeople and you are going to put together a sales contest to get them motivated. You have a first place, second place, and third place winner. If I am one of your sales team members what would I be thinking? "I already know who is going to win, they always win, so why put forth the effort?" You end up with 3 winners and 47 losers! You have just reinforced the fact that the majority of your salespeople are losers. To get your sales team motivated you have to do more than offer a simple contest, you have to offer a program.

You can get your team temporarily inspired by bringing in a "motivational speaker" and you may see a slight increase, however, it soon fades away. Here is the part that most people don't understand about getting a sales team inspired. Inspiration and opportunity never meet. Inspiration should be used to inspire salespeople to become more prepared by improving their selling skills and industry knowledge. Then preparation and opportunity will intersect and ignite into long term motivation.

## Have you ever used a KPI?

A KPI can be used as a great benchmark and motivator. It stands for Key Performance Indicator. Here's how it can be used as an effective management tool.

One of the toughest jobs for a salesperson to do is to stay focused. It seems like there are always things coming up during the course of a day that gets us off track. We end up wasting most of our time on the small things and don't get the important priorities done. By using well thought out KPI's it becomes easier to stay on track. However, here is a very important key in effectively using KPI's. Never have more that five, and never have less than five. If you were going to fill a bucked full of rocks, gravel and sand, you would have to put the big rocks in first. If you put the gravel and sand in first there will be no room left for the big rocks. The big rocks represent your 5 KPI's.

The second key in using KPI's is accountability. If you are a manager here is a great way to help keep your salespeople on track. Use a "Friday Report" system. Every Friday have each salesperson give a report on how they did during the week on their key performance indicators (KPI's). This can be simple and even given over voice mail.  You don't want to create something that requires more paperwork but something that creates accountability.

If you have 5 KPI's that the entire sales team is accountable for you can in turn pass along your combined Friday Report or summary to your manager. Your manager, in turn, can then give a summary of their sales performance up the chain of command until it reaches the top.  This keeps the entire sales team on the same page and everyone knows exactly what is expected.

**Here is a sample of 5 KPI's:**

**Sales** (Number of new account calls)

**New line items** (What products and what customer)

**Broker assistance** (Activity and results)

**Business reviews**   (Account and results)

**Collections** (Solutions or potential problems)

Give a short review every Friday with each salesperson, letting them know how they are doing.  This will let them know that you are paying attention to their performance in each of the five areas.  Pass this along all the way to the top and the entire company becomes focused.

Here is the problem with using this system.  Some overly creative manager will say "if 5 KPI's work so well why not have 10.  If leaving a voice mail with your DSM works so well why not have them fill out a report online".  Then the HR department will get a hold of it and make it into a huge performance evaluation review and increase the number to 40 KPI's.  Then they will discover that they already have this information in their file and wonder why it doesn't work.

**FIVE!  That's it!** If you can get everyone in the company focused on doing 5 things you will out-perform the company that is trying to do 40 things by at least 10 to 1.

This fits perfectly with another acronym **SMIR**.  The letters stand for **Specific, Measurable, Individual and Recognition**. If you tie the 5 KPI's to an SMIR program you have an unbeatable formula.  **KPI + SMIR = SUCCESS.**

## Recognition...

1  Why does unwarranted praise backfire?

2  What was the key ingredient Mary Kay used to start with $50 and exceed one billion in sales?

3  What was a key ingredient that improved a class of third grade students to improve their test scores by 75%?

4  What slogan did an insurance company use to double the sales of their agents?

5  Salespeople need an answer to what very important personal question?

6  Do salespeople ever get tired of being told that you think they can do something really special?

## Praise and recognition

As a manager and motivator why is praise and recognition so important?

There's really nothing you can do that's more important or will help your people more than letting salespeople know that you think they have great potential. The results will always be positive.

**Why should your salespeople see you as working to help them?**

A effective sales manager understands that it's much more important for his or her people to receive recognition than for him or her to receive it. When the sales department does something special, give all the praise and all the credit to your salespeople.  You will get your share of recognition because you are their manager.  But your salespeople may be overlooked unless you point out their contributions.  That lets them know that you're working for their success, as well as your own. Never your salespeople think they are working just to help get a promotion or make big money.

**Why don't most salespeople expect to succeed?**

Maybe that has been their history. Maybe they've tried selling different lines and nothing worked out. Maybe they think all companies are going to cheat them and hurt them because they've been cheated and hurt in the past. Many salespeople have decided to expect the worst and save themselves from more disappointment.

**As a sales manager why should you have expectations of success?**

When you hire a new salesperson to come to work with you in your business, their success will depend on their expectations of themselves and on your expectations of them.

If they have the expectations of success they will probably succeed. If your salespeople expect failure they will probably fail. It's been proven over and over again that things will work out exactly as you see them working out. It's your responsibility as a manager to help your salespeople grow in a positive way. You have to let them know that you cannot tolerate negative thinking. You must let them know that you know they can win, and you won't accept anything less than their best.

Most people set certain expectations for themselves. These expectations are usually low. They don't have the confidence to set lofty goals, and they're afraid to move out of their comfort zone.

**How can you be more objective about the talents and potential of your salespeople than they are?**

You may be able to set goals for them that are still reachable, yet much higher than they'd ever set for themselves.

Everyone who works for you can contribute or you wouldn't have hired or recruited them in the first place.

Every time you help a member of your sales team to set a goal and it's reached; you've helped them build the confidence to reach for an even higher goal. If you let people settle for modest goals, you will wind up with average and ordinary people on your team instead of superstars.

**How can your salespeople be expected to rise to your level of expectation?**

Another person may be as responsible for a salespersons level of achievement as the person themselves. Some salespeople will seldom push to their limit with no one around to watch or encourage them.

Never feel like the goals and expectations of your sales staff are none of your business. They need you behind them to help push them forward. They'll never resent the fact that you think they can do great things. Constant encouragement leads to increased expectations. No individual will push as hard as he or she will with help and encouragement from another person.

**Does a salesperson ever get tired of being told that you think they can do something really special?**

You can never give too much encouragement. That applies to new salespeople just starting out and salespeople who have been around for a long time.

Praise, recognition and encouragement don't produce instant results. It may take months of telling a person how special he or she is before you see any development in their own expectations.

Every time you let your salespeople know that you believe they can succeed, you build a little bit more of that inner strength. You build a reserve that can be the difference between whether your people quit or stick it out until they win.

**Why should you let your sales team know that you expect them to be a winner?**

Nothing encourages people to work harder and produce quality results like having their accomplishments noticed and praised. Praise and recognition are the most powerful forms of motivation.

This kind of motivation used to be one of the best-kept secrets in business. It's often ignored in standard sales management training, but successful leaders have always known its value. People respond better to praise than to punishment.

We all have needs. We all want to feel good about ourselves and the work we do. We all have the need to feel that we belong to a group, the need to feel appreciated, and the need to feel that we are recognized for our effort.

As a sales manager, it's good business to always be looking for a way to help people fulfill their desire for encouragement and recognition.

People work for a lot of reasons - but one of the main things they want from their job is recognition and appreciation.

**Why does praising an individual affect the group?**

If you start praising for successful behavior, the person will want to get the same kind of recognition again. Everybody wants recognition for a job well done. They will be anxious to repeat the actions that gave him or her such good feelings of recognition and accomplishment.

Many people have believed that praise has some sort of magic power. Do you believe in miracles? Many medical doctors and scientists today believe in miracles, even if they cannot understand them. You can praise a weak body into strength, a fearful heart into peace and trust; shattered nerves into poise and power; a failing business into prosperity and success.

## How do animal trainers use this power?

Animal trainers pet and reward their animals with delicacies for acts of obedience. Children respond with joy when they are praised. Even vegetation grows better for those who love it.

No one seems to know Just how praise and recognition releases energy. But the fact that it does is common experience. Ever notice how, when someone pays you a sincere compliment, or thanks you for a job well done, your spirits seem to get a shot in the arm?

The lift that you get from praise is not an illusion. Neither is it just your imagination. In some way, unknown to science, actual physical energy is released.

Why do so few of us recognize just how very important it is to a salesperson to be given recognition?

The National Retail Association asked thousands of workers and managers to list, in order of their importance, the factors that they felt were of most importance to workers. "Credit for work" was the item that the workers themselves overwhelmingly rated number one. The managers rated the same item number seven.

When we give salespeople what they are hungry for, they are much more likely to give us what we want from them.

Try it on a salesperson and watch them immediately "perk up." Also notice how they automatically become more friendly and cooperative.

It has also been proved that praise actually enables students to make better grades. When students were told just before an examination, "You will have little trouble with this test. It is well within your abilities and intelligence" they made better marks than when their intelligence and ability were run down just prior to the test. Praising their ability increased their ability.

**Why does a commission plan without recognition seem empty?**

Commission plans that just hand out money to employees, as a "gift" from the boss, invariably fail. But where commissions, bonuses and profit sharing are based on merit, and as a means of recognizing a persons worth to the company, production always goes up.

When should you begin to develop the habit of encouraging people?

Don't wait until someone does something big or unusual to praise him or her. If your morning cup of coffee is good, tell whoever made it. You'll not only raise their spirits, but the chances are they'll try to brew the coffee even better tomorrow morning.

Every time you say the words "Thank you," and mean it, you are giving the salesperson credit - praising him or her for having done something you appreciate. Look for things you can thank them for.

**Don't take it for granted that people know you appreciate them - tell them.**

When you let people know you appreciate what they have done, it makes them want to do still more for you. Say those kind words. Let people know how you feel.

Always have a good word for people every time you see them. Let them know whenever you notice something they've done well.

Always be the person who's saying something good about somebody. Sometimes, you may have to look hard to find something to praise. But it's there, somewhere, because everybody has good qualities.

## How do your show appreciation?

Appreciation should be sincere. Say it as if you mean it. Put some feeling into it. Don't let it sound routine, but special. Those two little words, "Thank you," can be magic words in business if they are used correctly.

Look at the person you are thanking. If he or she is worth being thanked, he is worth being looked at and noticed.

Thank people by name. Personalize your thanks by naming the person thanked. If there are several people in a group to be thanked, don't just say "thanks everybody," but name them.

## How can you surprise people?

Recognition and appreciation is even more powerful when the person does not expect it, or necessarily feel that he or deserves it. Think back to some time when you got a nice "thank you" from someone where it never occurred to you that any "thanks" were in order and you'll see what I mean.

Work at thanking people. Consciously and deliberately begin to look for things to thank other people for. Don't just wait until it occurs to you. Do it deliberately until it becomes a habit.  Gratitude does not seem to be a natural trait of human nature.  When Jesus healed ten lepers, only one thanked him.  But are we very different?

**Why should you recognize the act rather than the person?**

When you recognize an act your praise is specific and is more sincere.  The best results are obtained if they know exactly what they are being praised for.  Praising the act rather than the person avoids charges of favoritism or prejudice.

Most salespeople feel uncomfortable if you say "You're a great salesperson." It makes them feel you are handing them a line.

But if you pick out something specific, he or she has done, they feel good about it.

Praise a person for their sales achievement and they will do more work.  Praise him or her for their behavior, and behavior will improve.  But praise merely as a person and you only increase his egotism and conceit.  Many children have been ruined for life by their mother constantly telling them, "You're the most wonderful person in the world." In fact, one reason most of us are so stingy with praise and compliments is the fear that we will give the other person a swelled head.

# Why salespeople quit.

Forty-six percent of everyone who leaves a job does so due to a lack of appreciation.

## How does the Mary Kay organization use recognition?

The foundation of the company is based on the premise that women were not given the amount of praise and recognition they deserved. A system of awards for the various levels were set up and the women who joined the company were motivated to achieve some outstanding results. They were not motivated by the money alone, but by the accomplishment of reaching an objective and being recognized for it. The highest level of achievement in the Mary Kay company is that of a diamond bumble bee. The reason it was chosen was that a bumble bee, because of its size and the small wings, should not be able to fly, however, it goes against nature and does something that is meant to be impossible. The diamond studded lapel pin signifies that this woman has done something that she shouldn't have been able to do.

At some of the company award banquets, many of the managers and salespeople would come up on the stage after it was over and get the feel of what it would be like to receive some of the awards, and then go back home working harder than ever to make it happen for them at the next banquet.

**A test done on students produced surprising results**.

A group of third grade students were used to see what effect praise and recognition would have on their work. The class was divided into two groups and given a math lesson. One of the groups were criticized every time they made a mistake and ignored when they did something right.

The other group was encouraged and praised every time they did something correct and when they made a mistake they were not criticized but encouraged to improve.

After the lesson they were given the same test to see if there would be difference.  Everyone was amazed when the results showed that the group who received the praise and encouragement did 75% better.

An insurance company had just completed the best year they ever had in their history, nearly doubling their sales for the year.

The new sales manager came up with a slogan for the year; "We Appreciate Our Agents". Then they set up a program to prove it. The entire support staff was told to go out of their way to make sure the salespeople out in the field were taken care of and made to feel important. They put together an incentive program that everyone could be a winner, not just the few top producers.

They took it a couple of steps further. At the start of the year they sent flowers to all the agent's wives and said they appreciate the long hours and evenings away from home. During the year they sent monthly cards to their wives showing the great trip they would be going on at the end of the year.

**Salespeople need an answer to this very important personal question: "What is in it for me?"**

As you put these strategies to use, you will find the job only half begun. This is not a cynical question. It is another way of asking: "How much am I worth?" As owner or manager, you ask yourself the same question? So do your employees. And you must provide answers for them as well as for yourself. What incentives will you give them?

To feel a part of the business and to be given an incentive, each salesperson must understand that he or she is free to contribute ideas. Management should encourage employee ideas and provide the necessary system for obtaining them. Suggestion boxes and idea-discussion employee meetings are a couple of possibilities. Encourage employees to think about problems of the business. Some excellent ideas for their solution may be forthcoming. As a sales manager, carefully consider all ideas, and if adopted, commend or reward the giver. If not adopted, a word of explanation and appreciation should always be given. Successful sales managers build good attitudes in their salespeople by keeping them well informed.

1. Sincere praise miraculously releases energy in the other person, perks him up physically, as well as giving his spirits a lift.

2. The person who is discouraged, doing sloppy work, or just hard to get along with is probably suffering from low self-esteem. Praise can act as a wonder drug to give his self-esteem a healthy shot in the arm, change his behavior for the better.

3.  Give others credit for what they do.  Show your appreciation of what they have done by saying "thank you.

4.  Be generous with kind statements.  Gratitude is not a common thing.  By being generous with gratitude, you make yourself a stand-out.

5.  Increase your own satisfaction and peace of mind by paying several sincere compliments each day.

## Managing salespeople

Only 5% of all salespeople will ever reach their potential, 95% will never be truly be successful.  What does it take to be successful?  In order to evaluate this question, it is first necessary to understand what "success" is and what all successful people have in common. It is probably safe to assume that anyone reading this wants to be more successful.

### What is a good definition of success?

By definition, success is the realization of a worthy goal. Success is different for every individual.  For some people, an annual income of $25,000 would be a success, for another it may be $250,000.  Whatever it may be for you, there are specific characteristics that you must have in common with other successful people in order to achieve true success.

### Why are goals the single most important factor in achieving success?

Without a realistic goal, you will never know when you have reached your success level. Successful leaders set goals.

The goals must be realistic, measurable and obtainable within the bounds of your own perception. As time passes, your goals can always be adjusted upward to reach your ultimate goal of success.  However, if your initial goal is to be worth $1,000,000 by the year end and you are currently only worth $100,000 with an annual income of $50,000 a year and this is November, you most likely will never be able to reach it and therefore, it is unrealistic.  Biting off a job in small portions makes the eventual achievement of the total task seem easier and manageable. Successful people constantly set goals, re-evaluate their goals and scale them upward toward even greater accomplishments.

**Why are the most successful people being those who set goals early in life?**

So many people never get anywhere in their lives because they don't know where they are trying to go. If you don't have a destination how are you going to make plans?  If you don't know where you're going, how are you ever going to help anyone else reach their destination?

Several years ago, there was a study done at Harvard University. The graduating class was polled, and it was found that only 3 percent of the class had any clear goals set for their future.  Twenty years later, the researchers followed up on that same graduating class. *The 3 percent who had clearly defined goals accomplished more and made more money than the other 97 percent combined!*

It makes sense that if you don't know what you want to do with your life, or what you want to accomplish, you won't ever establish a working plan of action.

**What type of goals do you need?**

To really move ahead, you need short-term goals and long-term goals.  You need to know where you want to be six months from now and two years from now ... even 10 years from now.

**Is it alright to change your goals?**

There's nothing wrong with making changes in your goals as you go along.  It's important to be flexible. The most important thing is to make a conscious choice about what you want to achieve and how you're going to get there.

Wherever you are in your career, stop right now and analyze what you want, what your goals are, and begin a specific plan to reach them.  Know what you want, and work toward it every day.  Have specific goals, and a specific plan for reaching them.

**What comes first - long range or short-range goals?**

The long-term goals are the big goals, and they come first. After you've decided on those, it's important to establish a series of short-term goals that will provide you with day-to-day motivation.  Set a time frame that gives you enough time to take some serious action but isn't so far off into the future that you are tempted to postpone the activity.

Short-term goals establish a sense of urgency; they provide you with a deadline in the near future that prompts action.

**What is the best way to get the feeling of success?**

Anyone can do anything for 90 days.  You might set a goal of opening 10 new accounts a month.  Make the decision to do whatever it takes to make those 10 sales a month for 90 days.  What you might not be able to keep up for two years, you can force yourself to keep up for 90 days.

At the end of that period you've got a great feeling about yourself.  You've accomplished something that will pay off financially, and you're ready to celebrate.  The special benefit is that, once you've proven to yourself that you can open 4 new accounts a month, your regular goal of one or two accounts will seem like a breeze.

**What do you need for goal setting to be effective?**

The magic of 90 days can work for anyone, if they really commit to the effort. Encourage your people to set 30-day, 60-day and 90-day commitments. It's human nature that you need a series of small victories on the way to achieving your big ones. The short-term commitment provides motivation and encouragement to keep pushing ahead.

In order for your goal setting to be effective, you need some system of reinforcement, some way of rewarding yourself. Short-term goals give you reinforcement. Nothing succeeds like success. The day you start setting goals, you're a day closer to success.

**What is the biggest reason people do not set goals?**

One of the biggest dangers to achieving your goals - procrastination. We all do it, so nobody thinks too much about it. But continually putting off goal setting is far more likely to result in failure than any event or incident that will happen to you once you're on your way.

**What is the best advice on setting goals and making plans?**

Do it today. Don't wait until tomorrow or next week. Don't think you're too busy or too tired right now.  The longer you put it off, the more settled you will get in your present situation, and the easier it will seem to just drift along where you are right now.

**At what age is it too late to set goals?**

Take the time today to get off by yourself and think about your goals and desires. No matter how old you are, it's not too late to set goals and achieve them.  Get serious about your future.  When you start seeing your goals turn into realities, you will wish that you had started planning and goal-setting years earlier!

To win, you've got to have ability and the right attitude. You've got to have toughness and determination.  But before anything else, you've got to have a dream.  Your dream is the glue that holds all the effort together.  It's the one thing that, once you have it, no one can ever take away from you.

**Why do people lose their enthusiasm?**

**Our world today is so competitive and so tough that young people starting out sometimes get a lot of hard knocks.** One of the saddest things today is that most people have stopped dreaming.   Before they've had a chance to develop their potential, they get beaten down by how tough it is. The enthusiasm they once had turns to bitterness, and they decide to just "settle" for whatever hand they are dealt.  The older people get, the more and more they forget how to dream; they think that dreaming is only for children, not adults.

To win in life, you've got to be a dreamer.  You have got to become excited about your life and your future.

What most people really need is to know that there's a chance - an opportunity - for their dreams to come true. Encourage your people to dream.   If you want something badly enough, you can achieve it.

**If people are sick of jobs - what are they looking for?**

People are sick of jobs; they've had other jobs.  And many times, they've not been good experiences. All they want is a chance.  They don't want you to just offer them a job, they want you to offer them a dream and the opportunity to make it come true.  If you can offer people a chance to do something special with their lives, a chance to believe in something, a chance to dream again, you have given them the kind of motivation to succeed that they will never have if you just give them a set of duties.

**What is the one thing that will give you the "edge"?**

Never underestimate the power of dreaming.  Having a dream to strive for just may be the one quality that gives you that "edge" over most ordinary people.  We've all heard the expression that someone "has his or her heart set" on something. All your success, and the success of your people is, in the end, built on desire.  No matter what the odds are against you, if you've "set your heart" on something, you will have the determination and the motivation to see it through to the end.

**What do all successful people have in common?**

Encourage the dreams of your people.  Once you've got a dream, you can set goals, build your plans, and act. All great people are dreamers ... some let dreams die, but others nourish and protect them, nurse them through bad days. Goals are not just for business, but for all areas of your life. If you can see it, you can achieve it. Goals help you see where you're going and how you can get there.

## What is the primary duty of management?

Ask any group of workers, "What is the primary duty of management?" The answer setting goals is likely to be near the top of the list. If setting goals appears near the bottom of the list, you know there's a problem! In most companies, top management sets the overall direction of the organization. Middle managers then get the job of developing goals and plans for achieving the direction set by top management. Managers and employees work together to set goals and develop schedules for attaining them.

## How are goals used to benchmark progress?

To get something done, you have to set a definite vision - a target to aim for and to guide the efforts of you and your company. Goals provide direction. You can then translate this vision into goals that take you where you want to go. With goals, you can focus your efforts and the efforts of your staff on only the activities that move you toward where you're going.

Goals provide milestones to accomplishing your vision. Goals tell you how far you have traveled. Goals enable you to achieve your overall vision by dividing your efforts into smaller pieces that, when accomplished individually, add up to big results.

**What are the ingredients of effective goals?**

Once you get into a habit of goal setting, you will wonder how you ever managed to accomplish anything before. As far as your people are concerned, helping them establish their goals will be one of the most helpful things that you can do for them as a sales manager.

The best goals are SMART goals. SMART is a shorthand for the five characteristics of well-designed goals.

**Why should goals be specific?**

Goals must be clear and unambiguous; vagaries and platitudes have no place in goal setting. When goals are specific, they tell employees exactly what is expected, when, and how much. Because the goals are specific, you can easily measure your employees' progress toward their completion.

## Why should goals be measurable?

What good is a goal that you can't measure? If your goals are not measurable, you never know whether your employees are making progress toward their successful completion. Not only that, but it's tough for your employees to stay motivated to complete their goals when they have no milestones to indicate their progress.

## Why should goals be attainable?

Goals must be realistic and attainable by average employees. The best goals require employees to stretch a bit to achieve them, but they aren't extreme. That is, the goals are neither out of reach nor below standard performance. Goals that are set too high or too low become meaningless, and employees naturally come to ignore them.

## Why should goals be relevant?

Goals must be an important tool in the grand scheme of reaching your company's vision and mission. Eighty percent of worker productivity comes from only 20 percent of their activities. You can guess where the other 80 percent of work activity ends up! Relevant goals address the 20 percent of worker activities that has such a great impact on performance and brings your organization closer to its vision.

**Why should goals have a time limit?**

Goals must have starting points, ending points, and fixed duration. Commitment to deadlines helps employees to focus their efforts on completion of the goal on or before the due date. Goals without deadlines or schedules for completion tend to be overtaken by the day-to-day crises that invariably arise in an organization.

## What type of goals

By developing SMART goals with your employees, you can avoid these traps while ensuring the progress of your organization and its employees. Many sales managers neglect to work with their salespeople to set goals together. The ones that do, goals are often unclear, ambiguous, unrealistic, unrelated to the organization's vision, not measurable, and demotivating.

Although the SMART system of goal setting provides guidelines to help you frame effective goals, you have additional considerations to keep in mind. These considerations help you ensure that the goals, which you and your salespeople agree to, can be easily understood and acted on by anyone in your organization.

### How complex should goals be?

The easier your goals are to understand, the more likely the employees are to work to achieve them. Goals should be no longer than one sentence, and they should be concise, compelling, and easy to read and understand.

Goals that take more than a sentence to describe are actually multiple goals. When you find multiple-goal statements, break them into single, one-sentence goals. Goals should never take more than a page to describe.

**Why isn't it always better to have more goals?**

The greater the number of goals, the less you can focus on any one of them and the less you actually get done. No matter how great a manager or employee you are, you can't focus on everything at once.

**What goals have the greatest relevance to your success?**

Pick one to two goals to focus on. You can't do everything at once, and you can't expect your employees to either. A few goals are the most you should attempt to conquer at any one time.

Pick the goals with the greatest relevance (For example: sales - gross profit - new accounts - drop size - days outstanding). Certain goals take you a lot farther down the road to attaining your vision than do other goals. Because you have only so many hours in your workday, it clearly makes sense to concentrate your efforts on a few goals that have the biggest payoff - rather than on many goals with relatively less payoff.

**What is the best way to monitor the progress of your salespeople?**

The best way to monitor the progress of your salespeople is to first, clearly define their goals in each of the five area's: Sales, Gross profit,  Drop size,  New accounts, Collections

And second, have them give you a weekly report.  This weekly report can be a summary of their progress towards their five objectives.  The report can be delivered via voice mail, fax, email or in person over the phone.

## Your goal as a sales manager

As a manager your primary goal in measuring and monitoring the performance of salespeople is to help your team stay on schedule and to find out whether they need additional assistance or resources to do so. Few salespeople like to admit that they need help getting an assignment done - whatever the reason. Because of their reluctance, it's critical that you systematically check on their progress and regularly give them feed-back on how they are doing.

**If you don't monitor it, they won't achieve it.**

Don't leave achieving your goals to chance; develop systems to monitor progress and ensure that your salespeople are achieving them.

When you quantify a goal in precise numerical terms, your employees have no confusion over how their performance is measured and when their performance is adequate (or less than adequate).

**Why is positive feedback so important?**

**The secret to performance measuring and monitoring is the power of positive feedback.**

When you give positive feedback, you encourage the performance of the behavior that you want. However, when you give negative feedback you aren't encouraging the behavior you want; you are only discouraging the behaviors that you don't want.

## Constructive Criticism

**The most acceptable form of punishment is lack of praise**.

This method is much more powerful than criticism. If you withhold praise, you let the person know that he's not one of the leaders. If you're someone who constantly gives praise, hell know he's doing poorly when you stop praising, just as much as he would if you criticized him. You've let him know that he's not on the winning team right now, yet you haven't berated him or said anything negative.

When you feel like criticizing, don't. Spend your time making heroes out of other people. Give the people who are doing the job more attention. Before you know it, the poor performer will be dying to get back into the group that's getting praise and respect, and he will improve his performance to do so. You will accomplish the same end without saying anything hurtful.

When you only single out poor performance, you make people feel bad. They're so down on themselves that they won't do anything. All you accomplish is convincing them that they can't do anything right, so there's no reason to try. And that's not what you wanted at all.

When we tell another person, "I'm telling you this for your own good," we're not.  We're telling him to bolster up our own ego by pointing out some fault in him.

There are times when you must address a problem directly.  How can you give constructive criticism without bringing up individual failures?  One good way to discuss a "negative" is in a group setting.  When several people are present, you can address problems without singling out any individual for criticism.  Even though your problem won't apply to all the people in the group, you can get your point across without embarrassing the person who is guilty of the problem.  At the same time you can single out individuals who have handled a situation well, put them in the spotlight, and let everyone see the kind of action that inspires praise and recognition.

One of the most common failings in managing people is the way that we (sometimes unconsciously) attempt to increase our own feeling of self-esteem by lowering the self- esteem of another person.  Chronic fault-finding, belittling the other person, nagging, are all symptoms of low self-esteem.

However, there are going to be times when the successful manager must point out errors and "correct" those working with him.  This is truly an art, and one that most would-be leaders fall down on.

Because the art of criticism is so little known the very word criticism leaves a bad taste in our mouths.  When we think of the word, we think of those men and women who have criticized badly.  We are apt to think of someone "jumping down our throat," "showing us up," humiliating us, beating us down.

**Be slow to criticize.**

When you work with people one-on-one, you can say 99 positive things and one negative thing, and the only thing they will remember is the negative. Your emphasis has got to be positive.  You've got to lift their strengths.  You must be slow to criticize.  I know you are thinking, "Isn't there any action I can take when someone is doing badly?  Can I just let it slide?"

You will never hear a pilot say, "He's always finding fault with my flying.  Why can't he say something good for a change"?

The real purpose of criticism is not to beat the other person down, but to build him up.  Not to hurt their feelings, but to help them do a job better.

A pilot coming in for a landing is a good example of successful criticism.  Frequently, the pilots flying must be criticized or corrected by the tower.  If he's off course, the tower doesn't hesitate to tell him so.  If he's coming in too low, he's told about it.  If he is going to overshoot the field, he is corrected.  Yet you will never hear of a pilot getting offended by this criticism.

**The person in the tower criticizes the act, not the person.**

The next time you must get someone back on the track, remember how the airlines "correct" their pilots.  Keep in mind that their criticism is not for the purpose of ego satisfaction, but to achieve an end result for both the airline and the pilot.  The man in the tower doesn't deal in personalities. His criticism is not blared out over loud-speakers but in strict privacy to the pilot's earphones.

He doesn't say, "Well, if that isn't a dumb way to come in for a landing." He just says, "You're coming in too low."

The pilot isn't asked to do something merely to please the boss. He has a selfish incentive of his own to take the criticism and benefit by it. He is not offended; he actually appreciates it.

All criticism could be given in the same spirit; if it were, equally good results would be achieved.

**1. Criticism must be made in absolute privacy.**

If you want your criticism to take effect, you must not engage the other person's ego against you. Remember your goal - to achieve some good end result - or get him back on target, not to deflate his ego. Even if your motives are of the highest, and you have the night spirit about criticizing the other person, remember it's how he feels that counts. The mildest form of criticism made in the presence of others is very likely to be resented by the other person. Justified or not, he feels he has lost face before his co-workers or associates.

**2. Preface criticism with a kind word or compliment.**

Kind words, compliments, praise, have the effect of setting the stage in a friendly atmosphere. It serves notice on the other person that you are not attacking his ego and puts him more at his ease. The natural reaction of a person "called in on the carpet" is to get set to defend his ego. A person with this defensive frame of mind is not receptive to your ideas. By praising a person, you bring out the best in them and they will understand you better when criticism is necessary.

How to use praise and compliments to open the other person's mind:

"Bill, that was a swell report you turned in. You certainly covered all the important factors. However, there was one thing. . . ."

"Mary, you have done excellent work ever since you joined our company. We appreciate your efforts along this line. There is one thought for improvement I know you would appreciate..."

Jim, you have always co-operated so well in the past. Is there any reason why....

"George, you certainly have been a good sales professional all these years. Do you know"

"I know from past experience that you are always looking for little ways to constantly improve your work.  It occurred to me that. . ."

## 3.  Make the criticism impersonal.

Criticize the act, not the person.  Here again, you can sidestep the other person's ego, by criticism of his actions or behavior, not his person.  After all, it's his actions that you are interested in anyway.  By pinpointing your criticism to his acts, you can actually pay him a compliment, and build up his ego at the same time:

"John, I know from past experience that this error is not typical of your usual performance."

## Successful Criticism

"George, the only reason I mention this is I know you can easily do better. It is not up to your usual high standard."

This way you actually build him up while pointing out his mistakes. Instead of telling him, "You're no good," you say in substance, "I think you're much better than this performance would indicate."

You let him know you think he is better than the error; that you expect him to do better. This in itself is a powerful incentive to "live up to" your expectation.

RIGHT:" You forgot to ask for the order."

WRONG:" Your selling needs a lot of improvement."

RIGHT: "Better check your addition on these figures."

WRONG: "Of all the stupid mistakes."

There may arise situations where it would be more diplomatic to point out the thing connected with a person, rather than the act of the person himself. For example:

"Fred, somehow or other the weekly report did not find its way up to the accounting office. (It is Fred's responsibility to send it up.) Do you know what happened to that report, Fred?" This, rather than "Fred, you didn't get the report up to the accounting office in time."

## 4. Supply the answer.

When you tell the other person what he did wrong - also tell him how to do it right. The emphasis should not be on the mistake, but the means and ways to correct the mistake and avoid a repetition or recurrence.

One of the biggest complaints of workers is, "I don't know what is expected of me. Nothing I do seems to please the boss, but yet I am never sure what he wants."

Nothing can lower morale in an office, plant, or home, quite so much as an atmosphere of general dissatisfaction without there being any clear defining of just what is expected. Most people are anxious to "do right" if you tell them what "right" is.

As one salesperson expressed it, "My boss is always finding fault, criticizing my work. All I know is my way of doing it is wrong. Yet he never tells me what 'right' is.

There is no standard to aim at. It's like shooting at a target in the dark, with no idea where the bull's-eye is. All I know is that regardless of the direction I aim, I always seem to miss."

## 5. Ask for cooperation; don't demand it.

Asking always brings more cooperation than demanding. "Will you make these corrections?" arouses much less resentment than, "Do this over, and for Heaven's sake, this time see that you get it right!"

When you demand, you place the other person in the role of slave and yourself in the role of slave-driver. When you ask, you place him in the role of a member of your team. Team feeling, the feeling of participation, gets much more cooperation than force.

It also makes a great deal of difference whether you put Your criticism on the basis of "I'm the boss, and you'll do it this way because I say so," or whether you put it on the basis of, "Here's what we're shooting for, and here's how you can help achieve that goal."

You'll get much further. if you give the other person a selfish incentive for wanting to change his actions, than if you merely issue an order that he do so.

## 6. One criticism to an offense.

To call attention to a given error one time is justified. Twice is unnecessary. And three times is nagging. Remember your goal in criticism: to get a job done, not to win an ego fight.

When you're tempted to drag up the past or rehash a mistake that is over and done with, remember the illustration of how the man in the tower criticizes the pilot to bring him in safely. He tells him what he is doing wrong now and once that is corrected and settled, it is forgotten. Neither does the man in the tower "hold it against" the pilot because he once actually made a bad landing.

It is just as silly and ineffective for you to keep dragging up past mistakes and harping on them.

Employers are not the only ones who make this mistake. Husbands and wives drag up mistakes and errors from the past that should be dead and buried. Parents dig up dead issues in dealing with children. This never helps the other person to do better in the present; in fact, it is more likely to have just the opposite effect.

## 7. Finish in a friendly fashion.

Until an issue has been resolved on a friendly note, it really hasn't been finished. Don't leave things hanging in air, to be brought up later. Get it settled. Get it finished. Bury it.

Give the other person a pat on the back at the end of the interview. Let his last memory of the meeting be the pat on the back, instead of a kick in the pants.

RIGHT: "I know I can count on you."

WRONG:" Don't let it happen again."

RIGHT: "I know you'll get the knack of it-keep trying."

WRONG: "You've either got to show improvement soon-or else."

## Conducting an Interview

Questions to ask on a Job Interview?

1  Is there such a thing as a "Born Salesperson"?

2  How long do you think it will take to become a true professional in sales?

3  How do you feel about accepting responsibility for someone else's mistakes?

4  What is your definition of "Value Added Selling?

5  What motivates you to keep doing the things that are necessary for success?

6  On a scale from 1 to 10 how well prepared are you when making a sales call?

7  On a scale from 1 to 10 how good are you about filing important pieces of information?"

8  What are some of the things you do to help control your expenses?

9  What is your biggest accomplishment and how long did it take to accomplish it?.

How to save $50,000 on your training cost and avoid expensive turnover by hiring the right person in the first place.

## 1  Is there such a thing as a "Born Salesperson"?

People who think there is such a thing as a "born salesperson" are very difficult to train.  They think that everything depends on luck or natural talent.  Nothing could be farther from the truth.  Successful salespeople are eager to learn, study everything they can get their hands on, attend sales meetings and seminars with enthusiasm. They understand that it takes hard work to be successful in selling.

## 2  How long do you think it will take to become a true professional in sales?

Learning to be successful in a business as complex as the foodservice industry takes more time than many people are willing to invest.  There are two timelines.  The first is 3 years. A person should not even make a decision about the business until they give it the 3 year test. The second timeline is 5 years. Once a person is in foodservice sales for more than 5 years, it is very unlikely they will ever do anything else for a living.

**3 How do you feel about accepting responsibility for someone else's mistakes?**

We are in a business that requires a chain of people doing their job efficiently. If something goes wrong along the way the salesperson is the one who takes the heat. It is easy to blame someone else, however, the salesperson has to be willing to take responsibility for someone else's mistakes. If they are unable to do it - the business will eat them alive.

**4 What is your definition of "Value Added Selling?**

We are selling products made by the same manufacturer, same labeling, and the same cost, as our competitor. The real value has to come from the salesperson. Value added selling is not looking at the product as much as looking at the service and attention-to-detail the salesperson is willing to give. The only true point of differentiation is the sales rep and the "extra value" is their relationship.

**5 What motivates you to keep doing the things that are necessary for success?**

A successful salesperson has to be self motivated. There is very little room in our industry for maintainers, for salespeople who are willing to settle for minimum orders without being hungry for more. Successful salespeople have to be willing to do the things they don't feel like doing. No one likes to go hunting around for a box of bacon on a Friday night for a customer when they would rather be watching a movie. It takes a special kind of personal motivation to be that kind of person.

**6 On a scale from 1 to 10 how well prepared are you when making a sales call?**

To effectively call on between 25 and 50 accounts every week with the intention of increasing business with all of them requires a minimum of 4 to 6 hours of intense planning every week. Friday afternoon or Saturday morning are the most important hours of the entire sales process. It is as important as putting together a battle plan as if fighting a war. A person who does not understand how to plan and the importance of putting together the details of each call they are going to make during the next week will never be on top of their business.

**7  On a scale from 1 to 10 how good are you about filing important pieces of information?**

The important pieces of information are not only details about the customers business but include all the personal data you can collect. Each customer should be treated as importantly as your best friend.  A successful salesperson should know their family, hobbies, goals, and even their dogs name.  Personal information is power, and a salesperson should be willing to take extreme measures to get it and use it.

# High cost of turnover

A high rate of turnover is costly for several reasons. One important reason is that the recruiting, hiring and training of salespeople require a considerable outlay of money. The trainee's salary and schooling, as well as the expense of taking high salaried executive personnel from their regular duties while they train and otherwise counsel the new salesperson. Turnover of an excessive nature is also costly to the company in other ways which are less apparent. For example, if one new salesperson after another is sent to deal with the firm's customers, it is likely to make a bad impression on them and consequently result in a loss of business to the firm.

## Causes of a high turnover

In order to cut down on both visible and less obvious costs incurred through a high turnover of salespeople, the sales manager needs, first of all, to find the cause of the turnover. The cause may be found in poor selection, poor training, poor supervision, poor compensation, or in a combination of these factors.

The primary cause of high turnover often lies in the poor selection of salespeople. If you don't have the right person to start with the most costly training in the world, the most careful and expert supervision possible, and the best system of compensation will be worthless in preventing a high rate of turnover, with its resulting high cost. Before considering other causes of high turnover, you should first be sure that you are making a proper selection of salespeople.

**Basic qualifications**

In selecting salespeople, the basic qualifications should be considered by the sales manager. In sales, good character in every sense of the term is necessary. The salesperson is an ambassador of the company. In fact, to many customers and prospective customers, the salesperson is the company; their impression of the company is their impression of the salesperson.

In conformity with the generally high standard of business ethics which prevail today, customers insist that those with whom they deal shall be reliable, truthful, fair, of high integrity, and good repute. It is also essential to the company that its salespeople are trustworthy, since they are sent into the field with no one to keep a day-by-day check upon them. Consequently, if they are unreliable, they may do their company irreparable harm.

It has been said that the recipe for success in selling is two parts personality and one-part brains. Although a differentiation of the two is difficult, traits of personality have certain characteristics which cannot be accounted for by either character or intelligence. Under traits of personality may be grouped such qualifications as individuality, dress, appearance, manners, voice, intuition, and sympathetic comprehension.

The term "tact," which is generally considered to be a primary qualification for sales, implies knowledge of human nature and the ability to cope with it. Tact is often dependent on education, as distinguished from native intelligence, since education serves to develop the personality and social skill necessary for a salesperson to meet and deal with certain types of customers.

A sales manager may have a policy to recruit and select experienced or inexperienced salespeople. Some sales managers prefer inexperienced people, provided that they meet certain qualifications. The reason for this is that the inexperienced person usually brings with him or her no previously gained prejudice.  Such people, as a rule, are young and fresh from school and are consequently easily handled.  Coming recently from educational discipline, they are accustomed to taking orders and learning from their superiors.  As a result, it is not difficult for the sales manager to train people of this kind in the manner in which he or she wishes them to be trained.

On the other hand, there are sales managers who prefer to hire salespeople with experience since they do not require a complete training program in the new job.  These sales managers feel that experience is more than an offset to certain disadvantages.  For example, experienced salespeople may have prejudices which the sales manager must overcome.  In addition, such salespeople may have to unlearn certain ideas and methods before they are successful units of the new organization, able to sell in the way which the new company wishes them to sell.

Whether or not experience is to be one of the qualifications which a sales manager requires may depend on whether his concern is trying to break into new territory against keen competition.  Experienced people may be necessary to open a new market.  Once, however, such a market is established in a territory and the product is accepted, new salespeople may be able to bold the trade.

The question may arise as to whether or not the sales manager will attempt to hire the so-called "star." If a policy is adopted in connection with this matter, it means that a new salesperson must be qualified in a particular respect. Some sales managers believe that it is advisable to have in their organization one or two "stars" to act as pacesetters, even though these sales managers are aware of the fact that this may be the "star's" only value and a questionable one at that. As any competent track coach will admit, most pacesetters are not always capable of finishing the race. Furthermore, "star" salespeople generally have other drawbacks.

For instance, the "star" is likely to have a flair for one-way cooperation; the company must do everything for him or her and make allowance for all their eccentricities. In addition, he or she is prone to consider him or herself a privileged character not subject to rules and regulations and will probably want a better delivery schedule and the best credit terms for their customers. Reporting to the main office may be just a nuisance to this kind of salesperson and may consider it a waste of time to cultivate modest but potentially good customers. Finally, instead of stimulating the average salesperson, the "star" may discourage them because of his inability to keep up the pace set by the "star."

The qualifications required of a salesperson are sometimes set up for reasons of a more specific nature than the fact that they are dictated by the general policies of the company.

As an illustration you might set up certain rules to follow in the selection of salespeople.

College experience preferred.  It's equivalent if possible.

Previous selling experience preferred but not required.

Men and women without previous industry experience preferred.

Men or women who are not heavily in debt.

Applicants who cannot give good reasons for leaving previous jobs.

Those whose earnings have been higher than what they are willing to accept.

Applicants who have had five or more jobs in the last five years.

Applicants who have been less than two years on their longest previous job.

Gaps in applicant's employment history.

Attempts by the applicant to cover up or falsify items in his record.

Tendency of the applicant to blame others for his own failures.

Undue complaining or boasting on the part of the applicant.

Rate your salespeople 1 through 5 with 5 being the best.

___ Make sufficient number of new account calls

___ Account receivables are all within terms

___ Product knowledge is steadily improving

___ Account penetration is increasing

___ Product presentations are well prepared

___ Managing time and territory efficiently

___ Bring positive ideas to sales meetings

___ Make maximum use of marketing material

___ Becoming more of a partner with customers

___ Able to close sales without excessive pressure

___ Make use of supplier/broker/vendor assistance

___ Skilled in using computer as a selling tool

___ Enthusiastic response to customers needs

___ View obstacles as opportunities not problems

___ Able to make cold calls without fear of rejection

___ Make good use of the telephone for selling

___ Talk about all product categories with customers

___ Open to constructive criticism from DSM

___ Gross profit is within company goals

___ Attend professional sales training seminars


___ Total score 90-100 Great 80-90 Good 70-80 Get help!

**Contact me anytime**
**Bob@BobOros.com**

www.BobOros.com

## EVERYTHING A DSR NEEDS TO BUILD
## A TEN MILLION DOLLAR TERRITORY

## Ben Franklin's Little-Known Scientific
## Formula Improves Selling Skills 52%
*Designed for ongoing implementation*

**Paperback books as low as 8.00**

**Buy these six industry specific manuals for one low price.**

eBooks as low as 1.99 each

www.ingramcontent.com/pod-product-compliance
Lightning Source LLC
Chambersburg PA
CBHW030007190526
45157CB00014B/939